THE DOVER ANTHOLOGY
OF
BIRD POETRY

DOVER THRIFT EDITIONS

Edited by
NZ Kay

DOVER PUBLICATIONS
GARDEN CITY, NEW YORK

DOVER THRIFT EDITIONS

GENERAL EDITOR: SUSAN L. RATTINER
EDITOR OF THIS VOLUME: MICHAEL CROLAND

The Dover Anthology of Bird Poetry is a new work, first published by Dover Publications in 2024.

Library of Congress Cataloging-in-Publication Data

Names: Kay, NZ, editor.
Title: The Dover anthology of bird poetry / edited by NZ Kay.
Description: Garden City, New York : Dover Publications, 2024. | Series: Dover thrift editions | Summary: "Poets have long treated birds as a captivating source of inspiration as metaphors, references, and symbols of death, eternity, life, love, power, religious beliefs, and superstitions. Others have used different types of birds to express their thoughts and emotions. This volume highlights these remarkable creatures as they take flight from the Elizabethan era through the twentieth century. Selections from classic to contemporary authors include poems by William Blake, Emily Dickinson, John Keats, Herman Melville, Edgar Allan Poe, Wallace Stevens, William Carlos Williams, William Butler Yeats, and others. This anthology is ideal for classroom use, independent study, and personal perusal."—Provided by publisher.
Identifiers: LCCN 2023048553 | ISBN 9780486849287 (trade paperback)
Subjects: LCSH: Birds—Poetry. | BISAC: POETRY / Anthologies (multiple authors) | NATURE / Animals / Birds
Classification: LCC PN6110.B6 D68 2024 | DDC 808.81/93628—dc23/eng/20240221
LC record available at https://lccn.loc.gov/2023048553

Manufactured in the United States of America
84928701
www.doverpublications.com

Note

WE INTERACT WITH birds—big and small, wild and domesticated, dangerous and gentle, volant and flightless, glowingly gorgeous and awkwardly ugly—in varied ways, as admirers and predators.

Myriad beloved bards have tried their hand at composing poetry about birds and our relationships with them. In this alluring anthology, thirty-seven poets, spanning centuries, versify a menagerie of winged creatures with a variety of forms, styles, and tones. This collection vividly captures birds' beauty, song, and flight—and their very nature.

Avian poetry is more than just descriptions of and commentary about birds. The selections in this volume aren't the poetic equivalent of John James Audubon's ornithological paintings. Rather, bird poetry takes liberties, speaking to how humans see birds and, by extension, ourselves.

Birds are a rich source of metaphors. We seek to soar high like they can, and they inspired our efforts to construct aircraft and go where they could. We yearn to get a bird's-eye view of situations, which suggests an optimal perspective. We cherish birds' songs and craft our own, with our species initially imitating what we heard from the beasts in the skies and the trees. Birds can represent such opposite concepts as freedom and captivity.

With contributions by top-tier writers encompassing such diverse approaches as horror, nonsense verse, religious poetry, and sonnets, *The Dover Anthology of Bird Poetry* presents a wide wingspan of avian tributes and reflections.

Contents

Contents

Introduction

EXISTENCE IS MEASURED through perception. We see and we hear. We process and we learn. Eventually we are present. And when we grow too weary from it, our bodies lay down in the cold and cease to be. The space between points we litter with screaming, abrasion, closets and violence. We are made hoarse, ragged from chastising the great vacuity and the rain for every affliction we nailed our hands to as our ever-interrupted spirits are yanked heart-first, yoked to sparrows, hurdling toward the sun. Forever is the prisoner of her wisdom. Eternity flees her by the hour. We are blessed, doomed to carry on never understanding a single thing she's ever saying, except it to us is a song of endless wonder, built of better things.

The bird is that rare creature which, like us, acts as both vehicle and witness to the everyday miracle of living. They are a constant melody and image. We hear them. We collect them. We demand they sing for us. Concocted origins and philosophic riddles surround them. The same world at the same time happens to them, but they proclaim every joy man was built not to know. Our poetry of the situation is a cope aesthetic, ravaged by ancient morality, grim naturalism, beatific medievalism, and transcendental exultation. The world of birds is vicious and complex. It is full of monsters and killers. It teems with amazing displays of grace, and casually reckless death. It is full of songs of love. Songs for dancing. Songs of carnage. They exit their world into ours as the originators of terror. They are the reason for cave-dwelling, subterranean fear. They are the emblem of the death from above we will never hear. Always silently timing every movement. Eyeing us from the green darkness of the trees as meat to be fed alive to their naked, shrieking issue at some breath-stealing climb. The birds have served as inspiration for every dream of flight, and every nightmarish penance the vengeful gods can bestow. They are faithful companions, and harbingers of dreadful days. Integral to every tale of battle is the

ancient and *honest clatter* of black wings. The ravens are unkind; the
owls conspire; the eagles gather; the vulture waits. They clear the fields
of battle. They have come to raze the dead. They are the set pieces of
a savage and residual blood memory from the too brutal origins of the
world, and a reminder of the role befalling all the victims of man. The
passenger pigeon slaughtered for hats. The dodo for lack of knowing
Jesus. The giant condor was too big to live. The nongeometric density
of the thing demands the consideration of a time beyond comprehension,
which our nearest approximation of is a horrendous lie. Yet, ultimately,
they have met man without his illusions; they have met his interpretations
and improvements; they have met him at his truest: as the eradicator.

The natural poetry we glean from the birds grows out of the grimness
of this relationship. It is an attempt through a less martial light to *turn
things to their proper channel again*. An attempt to, without hostile
intention, inspect the spirit as it relates to the environment. But it
cannot distance us from the inherent violence origination requires.

Maybe you've heard this one before: Which came first, the chicken
or the egg? And cue the laughter; cue the rolling of the eyes. But
the question is not illegitimate: It is unpleasant to deconstruct. How
were the birds domesticated? The world's not a bunch of Rocky
Balboas chasing down chickens, and there's no mass hypnosis calling
out around the world and disrupting the magnets in the pigeons. So
how? Nets and snares? The repurposing of tools to suit needs, the
need for fire, assumes a cleverer man than our protorat progenitors
were. We are watchers, and we have watched the birds for eternity.
They sit and nest, the eggs crack, and then there are more birds.
What do the snakes and the other reptiles eat? Eggs and carcasses.
And whose sad example are we doomed to repeat? So the egg came
first. The distraction and murder to steal the nest came shortly
afterward. To raise the hatchlings to produce more birds likely
followed. So the chicken isn't even second. It's not necessarily even
third. But from there we taught the birds about differences.

Our life with the birds is a tale of horror we disguise with praise
and pondering. We jest at them in wonder, perplexed by flight,
agog at their deftness and perfect arrangement of notes. The birds
have become intricate devices. Shared emotional contortions become
words placed together to produce an image in the color and spirit
of something unnameable about the past only allowed after life.
Even the mighty thunderbird is now a select member of that universal
troupe of monsters. Alongside Leatherface, the Wolf Man, Krueger,
and Voorhees stands the flightless atrocity of the Argonauts, the

terrible roc, the winged serpent Q spiraling along blue miles, Hitchcock's anonymous revolutionaries at watch from the wires, and the raven that never leaves the door. Birds aren't even real. They are uncanny, finely wrought objects. More maps and tools required to excavate a memory and craft a poem than living things. We arrange them in our failed attempts to explain the world as it was experienced. And that world is always uncertain, and recall is not absolute, but the birds make sturdy beams to trail in the darkness, to help recover what used to be there through their constancy; whether in living song and color or cadaver stillness, they lead us back to the beatific moment and aid in reassembling the epiphany. The birds are not there to be discovered, but instead exist in perpetuity throughout the songs of man, ever-present above us, and our opposite in all things. His first love. They make mean our attempts to express God's brilliance. We are at odds in composition. The day as it happens is for anyone listening, and they dip into it without fear. They lack the dreadful fetching mores of modern abstract discontent. They are without internal critic or peer. And while we are here, we will remain unable to understand the world of the birds. It is closed to us. At what point did we pick up that strange rock to sling and drop our brother able to live free—unburdened by the weight of His love—and eat his offspring, cage his females, and breed his generations into mutagenic deformity to satisfy some appetite learned from the unbearable monsters that stalked the iron cauldron of the Earth before the flood? If the last shredded note wrung from the throats of the great auks as their unborn cracked against the rocks wasn't the end of this world, or if the wild turkeys dream a dream of flight that makes the Wrights' discovery sad, we are incapable of hearing it; we are incapable of understanding. But crows do use crosswalks, and when she was dead and he was alone, the Kauaʻi ʻōʻōʼs dirge challenged the recorders in the silence, his private threnody sung for no one to hear.

The birds sing of and to the immortal beauty in a voice we may mimic and never decipher, so we write about them. We transform them into fixtures of the seasons. We make them caricatures of wisdom, instruments, like-prisoners of insecurity used as an examination of limits. And they strive against gravity, magnifying the beam, scattering light in a well-earned living fear of us, blithely avoiding our trouble as best as they're able. Where our tiny wings have spread they've learned to notice. Yet they remain a permanent metaphor for any iteration of interior speculation, any splendor in the mundane, any genuine exercise of faith, and the living thing as its most exact self. They are words of ancient meter that have told the centuries perfect synonyms for our wandering blue spirits in contortion over this belligerent and terminal reality. The leaden tears of Urizen sing careening and on fire across the banality of our limitless horizons, a tonic for the coming darkness, total immobility, and the cold ground. A proof against entropy, they are the living resistance to loss. We write about the birds because doing so lets us hold a fragile piece of the eternal in our hands. And anyone can do that. They only have to.

NZ KAY

THE DOVER ANTHOLOGY
OF
BIRD POETRY

William Blake

The Blossom

Merry Merry Sparrow
Under leaves so green
A happy Blossom
Sees you swift as arrow
Seek your cradle narrow
Near my Bosom.

Pretty Pretty Robin
Under leaves so green
A happy Blossom
Hears you sobbing sobbing
Pretty Pretty Robin
Near my Bosom.

The Fairy

"Come hither, my sparrows,
My little arrows.
If a tear or a smile
Will a man beguile,
If an amorous delay
Clouds a sunshiny day,
If the step of a foot
Smites the heart to its root,
'Tis the marriage ring—
Makes each fairy a king."

So a fairy sung.
From the leaves I sprung;
He leap'd from the spray
To flee away;
But in my hat caught,
He soon shall be taught.
Let him laugh, let him cry,
He's my butterfly;
For I've pulled out the sting
Of the marriage ring.

Thel's Motto

Does the Eagle know what is in the pit?
Or wilt thou go ask the Mole:
Can Wisdom be put in a silver rod?
Or Love in a golden bowl?

Thou hearest the Nightingale begin the Song of Spring

Thou hearest the Nightingale begin the Song of Spring;
The Lark, sitting upon his earthy bed: just as the morn
Appears; listens silent; then springing from the waving Corn-field!
  Loud
He leads the Choir of Day! trill, trill, trill, trill,
Mounting upon the wings of light into the great Expanse:
Reechoing against the lovely blue & shining heavenly Shell:
His little throat labours with inspiration; every feather
On throat & breast & wings vibrates with the effluence Divine
All Nature listens silent to him & the awful Sun
Stands still upon the Mountain looking on this little Bird
With eyes of soft humility, & wonder love & awe.
Then loud from their green covert all the Birds begin their Song
The Thrush, the Linnet & the Goldfinch, Robin & the Wren
Awake the Sun from his sweet reverie upon the Mountain:
The Nightingale again assays his song, & thro the day,
And thro the night warbles luxuriant; every Bird of Song
Attending his loud harmony with admiration & love.
This is a Vision of the lamentation of Beulah over Ololon!

Anne Brontë

The Captive Dove

Poor restless dove, I pity thee;
And when I hear thy plaintive moan,
I mourn for thy captivity,
And in thy woes forget my own.

To see thee stand prepared to fly.
And flap those useless wings of thine,
And gaze into the distant sky,
Would melt a harder heart than mine.

In vain—in vain! Thou canst no rise:
Thy prison roof confines thee there;
Its slender wires delude thine eyes,
And quench thy longings with despair.

Oh, thou wert made to wander free
In sunny mead and shady grove,
And, far beyond the rolling sea,
In distant climes, at will to rove!

Yet, hadst thou but one gentle mate
Thy little drooping heart to cheer,
And share with thee thy captive state,
Thou couldst be happy even there.

Yes, even there, if, listening by,
One faithful dear companion stood,
While gazing on her full bright eye,
Thou mightst forget thy native wood.

But thou, poor solitary dove,
Must make, unheard, thy joyless moan;
The heart, that Nature formed to love,
Must pine, neglected, and alone.

William Cullen Bryant

To a Waterfowl

Whither, 'midst falling dew,
While glow the heavens with the last steps of day,
Far, through their rosy depths, dost thou pursue
    Thy solitary way?

Vainly the fowler's eye
Might mark thy distant flight, to do thee wrong,
As, darkly seen against the crimson sky,
    Thy figure floats along.

Seek'st thou the plashy brink
Of weedy lake, or marge of river wide,
Or where the rocking billows rise and sink
    On the chaféd ocean-side?

There is a Power whose care
Teaches thy way along that pathless coast—
The desert and illimitable air—
    Lone wandering, but not lost.

All day thy wings have fanned,
At that far height, the cold thin atmosphere,
Yet stoop not, weary, to the welcome land,
    Though the dark night is near.

And soon that toil shall end;
Soon shalt thou find a summer home, and rest,
And scream among thy fellows; reeds shall bend,
      Soon, o'er thy sheltered nest.

Thou'rt gone, the abyss of heaven
Hath swallowed up thy form; yet, on my heart
Deeply hath sunk the lesson thou hast given,
      And shall not soon depart.

He, who, from zone to zone,
Guides through the boundless sky thy certain flight,
In the long way that I must tread alone,
      Will lead my steps aright.

Robert Burns

Address to the Woodlark

O stay, sweet warbling woodlark, stay!
Nor quit for me the trembling spray;
A hapless lover courts thy lay,
    Thy soothing, fond complaining.

Again, again that tender part,
That I may catch thy melting art;
For surely that wad touch her heart,
    Wha kills me wi' disdaining.

Say, was thy little mate unkind,
And heard thee as the careless wind?
Oh! nocht but love and sorrow joined,
    Sic notes o' wo could wauken.

Thou tells o' never-ending care,
O' speechless grief, and dark despair:
For pity's sake, sweet bird, nae mair,
    Or my poor heart is broken!

Lewis Carroll

Little Birds

Little Birds are dining
  Warily and well,
  Hid in mossy cell;
Hid, I say, by waiters
Gorgeous in their gaiters—
  I've a tale to tell.

Little Birds are feeding
  Justices with jam,
  Rich in frizzled ham;
Rich, I say, in oysters
Haunting shady cloisters—
  That is what I am.

Little Birds are teaching
  Tigresses to smile,
  Innocent of guile;
Smile, I say, not smirkle—
Mouth a semicircle,
  That's the proper style.

Little Birds are sleeping
  All among the pins,
  Where the loser wins;
Where, I say, he sneezes
When and how he pleases—
  So the tale begins.

Little Birds are writing
  Interesting books,
  To be read by cooks;
Read, I say, not roasted—
Letter-press, when toasted,
  Loses its good looks.

Little Birds are playing
  Bagpipes on the shore,
  Where the tourists snore.
"Thanks!" they cry. "'Tis thrilling!
Take, oh, take this shilling!
  Let us have no more!"

Little Birds are bathing
  Crocodiles in cream,
  Like a happy dream;
Like, but not so lasting—
Crocodiles, when fasting,
  Are not all they seem!

Little Birds are choking
  Baronets with bun,
  Taught to fire a gun;
Taught, I say, to splinter
Salmon in the winter—
  Merely for the fun.

Little Birds are hiding
  Crimes in carpet-bags,
  Blessed by happy stags;
Blessed, I say, though beaten—
Since our friends are eaten
  When the memory flags.

Little Birds are tasting
  Gratitude and gold,
  Pale with sudden cold;
Pale, I say, and wrinkled—
When the bells have tinkled
  And the tale is told.

John Clare

The Nightingale's Nest

Up this green woodland-ride let's softly rove,
And list the nightingale—she dwells just here.
Hush! let the wood-gate softly clap, for fear
The noise might drive her from her home of love;
For here I've heard her many a merry year—
At morn, at eve, nay, all the live-long day,
As though she lived on song. This very spot,
Just where that old-man's beard all wildly trails
Rude arbours o'er the road, and stops the way—
And where that child its blue-bell flowers hath got,
Laughing and creeping through the mossy rails—
There have I hunted like a very boy,
Creeping on hands and knees through matted thorn
To find her nest, and see her feed her young.
And vainly did I many hours employ;
All seemed as hidden as a thought unborn.
And where those crimping fern-leaves ramp among
The hazel's under boughs, I've nestled down,
And watched her while she sung; and her renown
Hath made me marvel that so famed a bird
Should have no better dress than russet brown.
Her wings would tremble in her ecstasy,
And feathers stand on end, as t'were with joy,
And mouth wide open to release her heart
Of its out-sobbing songs. The happiest part
Of summer's fame she shared, for so to me
Did happy fancies shapen her employ;
But if I touched a bush, or scarcely stirred,

12

All in a moment stopt. I watched in vain;
The timid bird had left the hazel bush,
And at a distance hid to sing again.
Lost in a wilderness of listening leaves,
Rich Ecstasy would pour its luscious strain,
Till envy spurred the emulating thrush
To start less wild and scarce inferior songs;
For while of half the year Care him bereaves,
To damp the ardour of his speckled breast;
The nightingale to summer's life belongs,
And naked trees, and winter's nipping wrongs,
Are strangers to her music and her rest.
Her joys are evergreen, her world is wide—
Hark! there she is as usual—let's be hush—
For in this black-thorn clump, if rightly guess'd,
Her curious house is hidden. Part aside
These hazel branches in a gentle way,
And stoop right cautious 'neath the rustling boughs,
For we will have another search to-day,
And hunt this fern-strewn thorn-clump round and round;
And where this reeded wood-grass idly bows,
We'll wade right through, it is a likely nook:
In such like spots, and often on the ground,
They'll build, where rude boys never think to look—
Aye, as I live! her secret nest is here,
Upon this white-thorn stump! I've searched about
For hours in vain. There! put that bramble by—
Nay, trample on its branches and get near.
How subtle is the bird! she started out,
And raised a plaintive note of danger nigh,
Ere we were past the brambles; and now, near
Her nest, she sudden stops—as choking fear,
That might betray her home. So even now
We'll leave it as we found it: safety's guard
Of pathless solitude shall keep it still.
See there! she's sitting on the old oak bough,
Mute in her fears; our presence doth retard
Her joys, and doubt turns every rapture chill.
Sing on, sweet bird! may no worse hap befall
Thy visions, than the fear that now deceives.
We will not plunder music of its dower,
Nor turn this spot of happiness to thrall;

For melody seems hid in every flower
That blossoms near thy home. These harebells all
Seem bowing with the beautiful in song;
And gaping cuckoo-flowers, with spotted leaves,
Seems blushing of the singing it has heard.
How curious is the nest; no other bird
Uses such loose materials, or weaves
Its dwelling in such spots: dead oaken leaves
Are placed without, and velvet moss within,
And little scraps of grass, and, scant and spare,
What scarcely seem materials, down and hair;
For from men's haunts she nothing seems to win.
Yet Nature is the builder, and contrives
Homes for her children's comfort, even here;
Where Solitude's disciples spend their lives
Unseen, save when a wanderer passes near
That loves such pleasant places. Deep adown,
The nest is made a hermit's mossy cell.
Snug lie her curious eggs, in number five,
Of deadened green, or rather olive brown;
And the old prickly thorn-bush guards them well.
So here we'll leave them, still unknown to wrong,
As the old woodland's legacy of song.

The Skylark

Above the russet clods the corn is seen
Sprouting its spiry points of tender green,
Where squats the hare, to terrors wide awake,
Like some brown clod the harrows failed to break.
Opening their golden caskets to the sun,
The buttercups make schoolboys eager run,
To see who shall be first to pluck the prize—
Up from their hurry see the Skylark flies,
And o'er her half-formed nest, with happy wings,
Winnows the air, till in the cloud she sings,
Then hangs a dust spot in the sunny skies,
And drops, and drops, till in her nest she lies,
Which they unheeded passed—not dreaming then
That birds, which flew so high, would drop again
To nests upon the ground, which anything
May come at to destroy. Had they the wing
Like such a bird, themselves would be too proud,
And build on nothing but a passing cloud!
As free from danger, as the heavens are free
From pain and toil, there would they build and be,
And sail about the world to scenes unheard
Of and unseen,—O were they but a bird!
So think they, while they listen to its song,
And smile and fancy and so pass along;
While its low nest, moist with the dews of morn,
Lies safely, with the leveret, in the corn.

Samuel Taylor Coleridge

The Nightingale

No cloud, no relic of the sunken day
Distinguishes the West, no long thin slip
Of sullen light, no obscure trembling hues.
Come, we will rest on this old mossy bridge!
You see the glimmer of the stream beneath,
But hear no murmuring: it flows silently,
O'er its soft bed of verdure. All is still,
A balmy night! and though the stars be dim,
Yet let us think upon the vernal showers
That gladden the green earth, and we shall find
A pleasure in the dimness of the stars.
And hark! the Nightingale begins its song.
"Most musical, most melancholy" bird!
A meloncholy bird? Oh! idle thought!
In nature there is nothing melancholy.
But some night-wandering man, whose heart was pierced
With the remembrance of a grievous wrong.
Or slow distemper, or neglected love
(And so, poor Wretch! filled all things with himself
And made all gentle sounds tell back the tale
Of his own sorrow), he and such as he,
First named these notes a meloncholy strain.
And many a poet echoes the conceit;
Poet who hath been building up the rhyme
When he had better far have stretch'd his limbs
Beside a brook in mossy forest-dell,
By Sun or Moon-light, to the influxes
Of shapes and sounds and shifting elements

16

Surrendering his whole spirit, of his song
And of his frame forgetful! So his fame
Should share in Nature's immortality,
A venerable thing! and so his song
Should make all Nature lovelier, and itself
Be loved like Nature! But 't will not be so;
And youths and maidens most poetical,
Who lose the deepening twilights of the spring
In ball-rooms and hot theatres, they still,
Full of meek sympathy, must heave their sighs
O'er Philomela's pity-pleading strains.

      My friend, and thou our Sister! We have learnt
A different lore: we may not thus profane
Nature's sweet voices, always full of love
And joyance! 'Tis the merry Nightingale
That crowds, and hurries, and precipitates
With fast thick warble his delicious notes,
As he were fearful that an April night
Would be too short for him to utter forth
His love-chant, and disburthen his full soul
Of all its music!
             And I know a grove
Of large extent, hard by a castle huge,
Which the great lord inhabits not; and so
This grove is wild with tangling underwood,
And the trim walks are broken up, and grass,
Thin grass and king-cups grow within the paths
But never elsewhere in one place I knew
So many Nightingales; and far and near,
In wood and thicket, over the wide grove,
They answer and provoke each other's song.
With skirmish and capricious passagings,
And murmurs musical and swift jug jug,
And one low piping sound more sweet than all—
Stirring the air with such a harmony,
That should you close your eyes, you might almost
Forget it was not day! On moonlight bushes,
Whose dewy leaflets are but half disclosed,
You may perchance behold them on the twigs,
Their bright, bright eyes, their eyes both bright and full,
Glistening, while many a glow-worm in the shade
Lights up her love-torch.

A most gentle Maid,
Who dwelleth in her hospitable home
Hard by the castle, and at latest eve
(Even like a lady vow'd and dedicate
To something more than Nature in the grove)
Glides through the pathways; she knows all their notes,
That gentle Maid! and oft a moment's space,
What time the Moon was lost behind a cloud,
Hath heard a pause of silence; till the Moon
Emerging, hath awaken'd earth and sky
With one sensation, and these wakeful Birds
Have all burst forth in choral minstrelsy,
As if some sudden gale had swept at once
A hundred airy harps! And she hath watch'd
Many a Nightingale perch'd giddily
On blossomy twig still swinging from the breeze,
And to that motion tune his wanton song
Like tipsy joy that reels with tossing head.

Farewell, O Warbler! till to-morrow eve,
And you, my friends! farewell, a short farewell!
We have been loitering long and pleasantly,
And now for our dear homes—That strain again?
Full fain it would delay me! My dear babe,
Who, capable of no articulate sound,
Mars all things with his imitative lisp,
How he would place his hand beside his ear,
His little hand, the small forefinger up,
And bid us listen! And I deem it wise
To make him Nature's Play-mate. He knows well
The evening-star; and once, when he awoke
In most distressful mood (some inward pain
Had made up that strange thing, an infant's dream),
I hurried with him to our orchard-plot,
And he beheld the Moon, and, hush'd at once,
Suspends his sobs, and laughs most silently,
While his fair eyes, that swam with undropp'd tears
Did glitter in the yellow moon-beam! Well!—
In a father's tale: But if that Heaven
Should give me life, his childhood shall grow up
Familiar with these songs, that with the night
He may associate joy! Once more, farewell,
Sweet Nightingale! Once more, my friends! farewell.

Olive Custance (Lady Alfred Douglas)

Peacocks: A Mood

In gorgeous plumage, azure, gold and green,
They trample the pale flowers, and their shrill cry
Troubles the garden's bright tranquillity!
Proud birds of Beauty, splendid and serene,
Spreading their brilliant fans, screen after screen
Of burnished sapphire, gemmed with mimic suns—
Strange magic eyes that, so the legend runs,
Will bring misfortune to this fair demesne . . .

And my gay youth, that, vain and debonair,
Sits in the sunshine—tired at last of play
(A child, that finds the morning all too long),
Tempts with its beauty that disastrous day
When in the gathering darkness of despair
Death shall strike dumb the laughing mouth of song.

Walter de la Mare

The Dove

How often, these hours, have I heard the monotonous crool
    of a dove—
Voice, low, insistent, obscure, since its nest it has hid in a grove—
Flowers of the linden wherethrough the hosts of the honeybees
    rove.

And I have been busily idle: no problems; nothing to prove;
No urgent foreboding; but only life's shallow habitual groove:
Then why, if I pause to listen, should the languageless note of a
    dove
So dark with disquietude seem? And what is it sorrowing of?

Emily Dickinson

In the Garden

A bird came down the walk:
He did not know I saw;
He bit an angle-worm in halves
And ate the fellow, raw.

And then he drank a dew
From a convenient grass,
And then hopped sidewise to the wall
To let a beetle pass.

He glanced with rapid eyes
That hurried all abroad,—
They looked like frightened beads, I thought;
He stirred his velvet head

Like one in danger, cautious,
I offered him a crumb,
And he unrolled his feathers
And rowed him softer home

Than oars divide the ocean,
Too silver for a seam,
Or butterflies, off banks of noon,
Leap, splashless, as they swim.

The saddest noise, the sweetest noise

The saddest noise, the sweetest noise,
The maddest noise that grows,—
The birds, they make it in the spring,
At night's delicious close.

Between the March and April line—
That magical frontier
Beyond which summer hesitates,
Almost too heavenly near.

It makes us think of all the dead
That sauntered with us here,
By separation's sorcery
Made cruelly more dear.

It makes us think of what we had,
And what we now deplore.
We almost wish those siren throats
Would go and sing no more.

An ear can break a human heart
As quickly as a spear,
We wish the ear had not a heart
So dangerously near.

A train went through a burial gate

A train went through a burial gate,
A bird broke forth and sang,
And trilled, and quivered, and shook his throat
Till all the churchyard rang;

And then adjusted his little notes,
And bowed and sang again.
Doubtless, he thought it meet of him
To say good-by to men.

Within my Garden, rides a Bird

Within my Garden, rides a Bird
Upon a single Wheel—
Whose spokes a dizzy Music make
As 'twere a travelling Mill—

He never stops, but slackens
Above the Ripest Rose—
Partakes without alighting
And praises as he goes,

Till every spice is tasted—
And then his Fairy Gig
Reels in remoter atmospheres—
And I rejoin my Dog,

And He and I, perplex us
If positive, 'twere we—
Or bore the Garden in the Brain
This Curiosity—

But He, the best Logician,
Refers my clumsy eye—
To just vibrating Blossoms!
An Exquisite Reply!

Ralph Waldo Emerson

Each and All

Little thinks, in the field, yon red–cloaked clown
Of thee from the hill-top looking down;
The heifer that lows in the upland farm,
Far–heard, lows not thine ear to charm;
The sexton, tolling his bell at noon,
Deems not that great Napoleon
Stops his horse, and lists with delight,
Whilst his files sweep round yon Alpine height;
Nor knowest thou what argument
Thy life to thy neighbor's creed has lent,
All are needed by each one—
Nothing is fair or good alone.
I thought the sparrow's note from heaven,
Singing at dawn on the alder bough;
I brought him home, in his nest, at even.
He sings the song, but it pleases not now;
For I did not bring home the river and sky:
He sang to my ear—they sang to my eye.
The delicate shells lay on the shore;
The bubbles of the latest wave
Fresh pearls to their enamel gave;
And the bellowing of the savage sea
Greeted their safe escape to me.
I wiped away the weeds and foam—
I fetched my sea-born treasures home;
But the poor, unsightly, noisome things
Had left their beauty on the shore,
With the sun, and the sand, and the wild uproar.

The lover watched his graceful maid,
As 'mid the virgin train she strayed,
Nor knew her beauty's best attire
Was woven still by the snow-white choir.
At last she came to his hermitage,
Like the bird from the woodlands to the cage;
The gay enchantment was undone—
A gentle wife, but fairy none.
Then I said, "I covet truth;
Beauty is unripe childhood's cheat—
I leave it behind with the games of youth."
As I spoke, beneath my feet
The ground-pine curled its pretty wreath,
Running over the club-moss burrs;
I inhaled the violet's breath;
Around me stood the oaks and firs;
Pine-cones and acorns lay on the ground;
Over me soared the eternal sky,
Full of light and of deity;
Again I saw, again I heard,
The rolling river, the morning bird;
Beauty through my senses stole—
I yielded myself to the perfect whole.

John Gould Fletcher

The Swan

Under a wall of bronze,
Where beeches dip and trail
Their branches in the water;
With red-tipped head and wings—
A beaked ship under sail—
There glides a single swan.

Under the autumn trees
He goes. The branches quiver,
Dance in the wraith-like water,
Which ripples beneath the sedge
With the slackening furrow that glides
In his wake when he is gone:
The beeches bow dark heads.

Into the windless dusk,
Where in mist great towers stand
Guarding a lonely strand,
That is bodiless and dim,
He speeds with easy stride;
And I would go beside,
Till the low brown hills divide
At last, for me and him.

Robert Frost

The Need of Being Versed in Country Things

The house had gone to bring again
To the midnight sky a sunset glow.
Now the chimney was all of the house that stood,
Like a pistil after the petals go.

The barn opposed across the way,
That would have joined the house in flame
Had it been the will of the wind, was left
To bear forsaken the place's name.

No more it opened with all one end
For teams that came by the stony road
To drum on the floor with scurrying hoofs
And brush the mow with the summer load.

The birds that came to it through the air
At broken windows flew out and in,
Their murmur more like the sigh we sigh
From too much dwelling on what has been.

Yet for them the lilac renewed its leaf,
And the aged elm, though touched with fire;
And the dry pump flung up an awkward arm;
And the fence post carried a strand of wire.

For them there was really nothing sad.
But though they rejoiced in the nest they kept,
One had to be versed in country things
Not to believe the phoebes wept.

The Oven Bird

There is a singer everyone has heard,
Loud, a mid-summer and a mid-wood bird,
Who makes the solid tree trunks sound again.
He says that leaves are old and that for flowers
Mid-summer is to spring as one to ten.
He says the early petal-fall is past
When pear and cherry bloom went down in showers
On sunny days a moment overcast;
And comes that other fall we name the fall.
He says the highway dust is over all.
The bird would cease and be as other birds
But that he knows in singing not to sing.
The question that he frames in all but words
Is what to make of a diminished thing.

Thomas Hardy

The Darkling Thrush

I leant upon a coppice gate

When Frost was spectre-gray,
And Winter's dregs made desolate

The weakening eye of day.
The tangled bine-stems scored the sky

Like strings of broken lyres,
And all mankind that haunted nigh

Had sought their household fires.

The land's sharp features seemed to be

The Century's corpse outleant,
His crypt the cloudy canopy,

The wind his death-lament.
The ancient pulse of germ and birth

Was shrunken hard and dry,
And every spirit upon earth

Seemed fervourless as I.

At once a voice arose among

The bleak twigs overhead
In a full-hearted evensong

Of joy illimited;
An aged thrush, frail, gaunt, and small,

In blast-beruffled plume,
Had chosen thus to fling his soul

Upon the growing gloom.

So little cause for carollings
Of such ecstatic sound
Was written on terrestrial things

Afar or nigh around,
That I could think there trembled through

His happy good-night air
Some blessed Hope, whereof he knew

And I was unaware.

The Selfsame Song

A bird sings the selfsame song,
With never a fault in its flow,
That we listened to here those long
Long years ago.

A pleasing marvel is how
A strain of such rapturous rote
Should have gone on thus till now
Unchanged in a note!

—But it's not the selfsame bird.—
No: perished to dust is he. . . .
As also are those who heard
That song with me.

William Ernest Henley

The Blackbird

The nightingale has a lyre of gold,
  The lark's is a clarion-call,
And the blackbird plays but a boxwood flute,
  But I love him best of all.

For his song is all of the joy of life,
  And we in the mad, spring weather,
We two have listened till he sang
  Our hearts and lips together.

George Herbert

Grieve Not the Holy Spirit

And art Thou grieved, sweet and sacred Dove,
  When I am sour,
    And cross Thy Love?
Grieved for me? the God of strength and power
  Griev'd for a worm, which when I tread,
  I pass away and leave it dead?

Then weep, mine eyes, the God of love doth grieve.
  Weep, foolish heart,
    And weeping live;
For earth is dry as dust. Yet if ye part,
  End as the night, whose sable hue
  Your sins express: melt into dew.

When saucy mirth shall knock or call at door,
  Cry out, Get hence,
    Or cry no more.
Almighty God doth grieve, He puts on sense:
  I sin not to my grief alone,
  But to my God's too: He doth groan.

O take thy lute, and tune it to a strain
  Which may with thee
    All day complain:
There can no discord but in ceasing be.
  Marbles can weep; and surely strings
  More bowels have than such hard things.

Lord, I adjudge my self to tears and grief;
        Even endless tears
            Without relief.
If a clear spring for me no time forbears,
        But runs, although I be not dry;
        I am no crystal, what shall I?

Yet if I wail not still, since still to wail
        Nature denies,
            And flesh would fail,
If my deserts were masters of mine eyes;
        Lord, pardon, for Thy Son makes good
        My want of tears with store of blood.

Man's Medley

Heark, how the birds do sing,
           And woods do ring.
All creatures have their joy, and man hath his.
        Yet if we rightly measure,
           Man's joy and pleasure
Rather hereafter then in present is.

        To this life things of sense
                Make their pretence;
In th' other Angels have a right by birth.
        Man ties them both alone,
           And makes them one,
With th' one hand touching heav'n, with th' other earth.

        In soul he mounts and flies,
                In flesh he dies.
He wears a stuffe whose thread is course and round,
        But trimm'd with curious lace,
           And should take place
After the trimming, not the stuffe and ground.

        Not that he may not here
                Taste of the cheer,
But as birds drink, and straight lift up their head,
        So he must sip and think
           Of better drink
He may attain to after he is dead.

        But as his joyes are double,
                So is his trouble.
He hath two winters, other things but one.
        Both frosts and thoughts do nip
           And bite his lip,
And he of all things fears two deaths alone.

Yet ev'n the greatest griefs
May be reliefs,
Could he but take them right, and in their wayes.
Happie is he, whose heart
Hath found the art
To turn his double pains to double praise.

Whitsunday

Listen, sweet Dove, unto my song,
And spread Thy golden wings in me;
Hatching my tender heart so long,
Till it get wing, and flie away with Thee.

Where is that fire which once descended
On Thy Apostles? Thou didst then
Keep open house, richly attended,
Feasting all comers by twelve chosen men.

Such glorious gifts Thou didst bestow,
That the earth did like a heaven appear;
The stars were coming down to know
If they might mend their wages, and serve here.

The sun, which once did shine alone,
Hung down his head, and wisht for night,
When he beheld twelve suns for one
Going about the world, and giving light.

But since those pipes of gold, which brought
That cordial water to our ground,
Were cut and martyr'd by the fault
Of those who did themselves through their side wound;

Thou shutt'st the door, and keep'st within;
Scarce a good joy creeps through the chink;
And if the braves of conquering sin
Did not excite Thee, we should wholly sink.

Lord, though we change, Thou art the same,
The same sweet God of love and light:
Restore this day, for Thy great Name,
Unto His ancient and miraculous right.

Gerard Manley Hopkins

The Windhover

I caught this morning morning's minion, king-
    dom of the daylight's dauphin, dapple-dawn-drawn Falcon,
      in his riding
    Of the rolling level underneath him steady air, and striding
High there, how he rung upon the rein of a wimpling wing
In his ecstacy! then off, off forth on swing,
    As a skate's heel sweeps smooth on a bow-bend: the hurl
      and gliding
    Rebuffed the big wind. My heart in hiding
Stirred for a bird,—the achieve of, the mastery of the thing!

Brute beauty and valour and act, oh, air, pride, plume, here
    Buckle! AND the fire that breaks from thee then, a billion
Times told lovelier, more dangerous, O my chevalier!

    No wonder of it: shéer plód makes plough down sillion
Shine, and blue-bleak embers, ah my dear,
    Fall, gall themselves, and gash gold-vermillion.

John Keats

Ode to a Nightingale

My heart aches, and a drowsy numbness pains
  My sense, as though of hemlock I had drunk,
Or emptied some dull opiate to the drains
  One minute past, and Lethe-wards had sunk:
'Tis not through envy of thy happy lot,
  But being too happy in thine happiness,—
      That thou, light-winged Dryad of the trees,
          In some melodious plot
Of beechen green, and shadows numberless,
      Singest of summer in full-throated ease.

O, for a draught of vintage! that hath been
  Cool'd a long age in the deep-delved earth,
Tasting of Flora and the country green,
  Dance, and Provençal song, and sunburnt mirth!
O for a beaker full of the warm South,
  Full of the true, the blushful Hippocrene,
      With beaded bubbles winking at the brim,
          And purple-stained mouth;
That I might drink, and leave the world unseen,
      And with thee fade away into the forest dim:

Fade far away, dissolve, and quite forget
  What thou among the leaves hast never known,
The weariness, the fever, and the fret
  Here, where men sit and hear each other groan;
Where palsy shakes a few, sad, last gray hairs,
  Where youth grows pale, and spectre-thin, and dies;
      Where but to think is to be full of sorrow
          And leaden-eyed despairs,
  Where Beauty cannot keep her lustrous eyes,
      Or new Love pine at them beyond to-morrow.

Away! away! for I will fly to thee,
  Not charioted by Bacchus and his pards,
But on the viewless wings of Poesy,
  Though the dull brain perplexes and retards:
Already with thee! tender is the night,
  And haply the Queen-Moon is on her throne,
      Cluster'd around by all her starry Fays;
          But here there is no light,
  Save what from heaven is with the breezes blown
      Through verdurous glooms and winding mossy ways.

I cannot see what flowers are at my feet,
  Nor what soft incense hangs upon the boughs,
But, in embalmed darkness, guess each sweet
  Wherewith the seasonable month endows
The grass, the thicket, and the fruit-tree wild;
  White hawthorn, and the pastoral eglantine;
      Fast fading violets cover'd up in leaves;
          And mid-May's eldest child,
  The coming musk-rose, full of dewy wine,
      The murmurous haunt of flies on summer eves.

Darkling I listen; and, for many a time
  I have been half in love with easeful Death,
Call'd him soft names in many a mused rhyme,
  To take into the air my quiet breath;
      Now more than ever seems it rich to die,
  To cease upon the midnight with no pain,
      While thou art pouring forth thy soul abroad
          In such an ecstasy!
  Still wouldst thou sing, and I have ears in vain—
      To thy high requiem become a sod.

Thou wast not born for death, immortal Bird!
  No hungry generations tread thee down;
The voice I hear this passing night was heard
  In ancient days by emperor and clown:
Perhaps the self-same song that found a path
  Through the sad heart of Ruth, when, sick for home,
      She stood in tears amid the alien corn;
          The same that oft-times hath
  Charm'd magic casements, opening on the foam
      Of perilous seas, in faery lands forlorn.

Forlorn! the very word is like a bell
  To toll me back from thee to my sole self!
Adieu! the fancy cannot cheat so well
  As she is fam'd to do, deceiving elf.
Adieu! adieu! thy plaintive anthem fades
  Past the near meadows, over the still stream,
      Up the hill-side; and now 'tis buried deep
          In the next valley-glades:
  Was it a vision, or a waking dream?
      Fled is that music:—Do I wake or sleep?

What the Thrush Said

O thou whose face hath felt the Winter's wind,
  Whose eye has seen the snow-clouds hung in mist,
  And the black elm tops 'mong the freezing stars
  To thee the spring will be a harvest-time.
O thou, whose only book has been the light
  Of supreme darkness which thou feddest on
  Night after night when Phœbus was away,
  To thee the Spring shall be a triple morn.
O fret not after knowledge—I have none,
  And yet my song comes native with the warmth.
O fret not after knowledge—I have none,
  And yet the Evening listens. He who saddens
At thought of idleness cannot be idle,
And he's awake who thinks himself asleep.

Charles Lamb

On the Sight of Swans in Kensington Garden

Queen-bird that sittest on thy shining-nest,
And thy young cygnets without sorrow hatchest,
And thou, thou other royal bird, that watchest
Lest the white mother wandering feet molest:
Shrined are your offspring in a crystal cradle,
Brighter than Helen's ere she yet had burst
Her shelly prison. They shall be born at first
Strong, active, graceful, perfect, swan-like, able
To tread the land or waters with security.
Unlike poor human births, conceived in sin,
In grief brought forth, both outwardly and in
Confessing weakness, error, and impurity.
Did heavenly creatures own succession's line,
The births of heaven like to yours would shine.

D. H. Lawrence

Humming-Bird

I can imagine, in some other world
Primeval-dumb, far back
In that most awful stillness, that only gasped and hummed,
Humming-birds raced down the avenues.

Before anything had a soul,
While life was a heave of Matter, half inanimate,
This little bit chipped off in brilliance
And went whizzing through the slow, vast, succulent stems.

I believe there were no flowers, then,
In the world where the humming-bird flashed ahead of creation.
I believe he pierced the slow vegetable veins with his long beak.

Probably he was big
As mosses, and little lizards, they say were once big.
Probably he was a jabbing, terrifying monster.

We look at him through the wrong end of the long telescope
    of Time,
Luckily for us.

Edward Lear

O Brother Chicken! Sister Chick!

O Brother Chicken! Sister Chick!
O gracious me! O my!
This broken Eggshell was my home!
I see it with my eye!
However did I get inside? Or how did I get out?
And must my life be evermore, an atmosphere of doubt?

Can no one tell? Can no one solve, this mystery of Eggs?
Or why we chirp and flap our wings,—or why we've all two legs?
And since we cannot understand,—
May it not seem to me,
That we were merely born by chance,
Egg-nostics for to be?

The Pelican Chorus

King and Queen of the Pelicans we;
No other Birds so grand we see!
None but we have feet like fins!
With lovely leathery throats and chins!
    Ploffskin, Pluffskin, Pelican jee!
    We think no Birds so happy as we!
    Plumpskin, Ploshkin, Pelican jill!
    We think so then, and we thought so still!

We live on the Nile. The Nile we love.
By night we sleep on the cliffs above;
By day we fish, and at eve we stand
On long bare islands of yellow sand,
And when the sun sinks slowly down,
And the great rock walls grow dark and brown,
Where the purple river rolls fast and dim
And the Ivory Ibis starlike skim,
Wing to wing we dance around,
Stamping our feet with a flumpy sound,
Opening our mouths as Pelicans ought;
And this is the song we nightly snort,—
    Ploffskin, Pluffskin, Pelican jee!
    We think no Birds so happy as we!
    Plumpskin, Ploshkin, Pelican jill!
    We think so then, and we thought so still!

Last year came out our Daughter Dell,
And all the Birds received her well.
To do her honor a feast we made
For every bird that can swim or wade,
Herons and Gulls, and Cormorants black,
Cranes, and flamingoes with scarlet back,
Plovers and Storks, and Geese in clouds,
Swans and Dilberry Ducks in crowds:
Thousands of Birds in wondrous flight!
They ate and drank and danced all night,
And echoing back from the rocks you heard
Multitude-echoes from Bird and Bird,—
    Ploffskin, Pluffskin, Pelican jee!
    We think no Birds so happy as we!
    Plumpskin, Ploshkin, Pelican jill!
    We think so then, and we thought so still!

Yes, they came; and among the rest,
The King of the Cranes all grandly dressed.
Such a lovely tail! Its feathers float
Between the ends of his blue dress-coat;
With pea-green trowsers all so neat,
And a delicate frill to hide his feet
(For though no one speaks of it, every one knows
He has got no webs between his toes!)

As soon as he saw our Daughter Dell,
In violent love that Crane King fell,—
On seeing her waddling form so fair,
With a wreath of shrimps in her short white hair.
And before the end of the next long day
Our Dell had given her heart away;
For the King of the Cranes had won that heart
With a Crocodile's egg and a large fish-tart.
She vowed to marry the King of the Cranes,
Leaving the Nile for stranges plains;
And away they flew in a gathering crowd
Of endless birds in a lengthening cloud.
    Ploffskin, Pluffskin, Pelican jee!
    We think no Birds so happy as we!
    Plumpskin, Ploshkin, Pelican jill!
    We think so then, and we thought so still!

And far away in the twilight sky
We heard them singing a lessening cry,—
Farther and farther, till out of sight,
And we stood alone in the silent night!
Often since, in the nights of June,
We sit on the sand and watch the moon,—
She has gone to the great Gromboolian Plain,
And we probably never shall meet again!
Oft, in the long still nights of June,
We sit on the rocks and watch the moon,—
She dwells by the streams of the Chankly Bore.
And we probably never shall see her more.

    Ploffskin, Pluffskin, Pelican jee!
    We think no Birds so happy as we!
    Plumpskin, Ploshkin, Pelican jill!
    We think so then, and we thought so still!

Turkey Discipline

Horrid Turkeys! what a pother!
Leave my Mother's gulls alone!
We, alas! can get no other,
If those precious two are gone!—
Still you persevere!—You Monsters!—
Over you have come—pell-mell!—
Oh! my gulls!—if you come near them
I will utter such a yell!!!

"Bless my heart—nine monstrous turkeys!—
Gracious!—all the garden's full!—
And one great one with a jerk has
Pounced upon my favourite gull!"
—Through the noise of turkeys calling,
Now was heard, distinct and well,
From the Southern window squalling
Many a long and awful yell.

Down rushed Fanny and Eliza;—
—Screams and squeaks and yowlings shrill,—
—Gulls and turkeys with their cries around them echoed o'er the
    hill:—
What would they not give to fetch them
Such a blow!—sad to tell—
As poor Fanny ran to catch them,
Evil turkeys—down she fell!—

Henry Wadsworth Longfellow

The Birds of Killingworth

It was the season, when through all the land
  The merle and mavis build, and building sing
Those lovely lyrics, written by His hand,
  Whom Saxon Caedmon calls the Blitheheart King;
When on the boughs the purple buds expand,
  The banners of the vanguard of the Spring,
And rivulets, rejoicing, rush and leap,
And wave their fluttering signals from the steep.

The robin and the bluebird, piping loud,
  Filled all the blossoming orchards with their glee;
The sparrows chirped as if they still were proud
  Their race in Holy Writ should mentioned be;
And hungry crows assembled in a crowd,
  Clamored their piteous prayer incessantly,
Knowing who hears the ravens cry, and said:
"Give us, O Lord, this day our daily bread!"

Across the Sound the birds of passage sailed,
  Speaking some unknown language strange and sweet
Of tropic isle remote, and passing hailed
  The village with the cheers of all their fleet;
Or quarrelling together, laughed and railed
  Like foreign sailors, landed in the street
Of seaport town, and with outlandish noise
Of oaths and gibberish frightening girls and boys.

51

Thus came the jocund Spring in Killingworth,
  In fabulous days; some hundred years ago;
And thrifty farmers, as they tilled the earth,
  Heard with alarm the cawing of the crow,
That mingled with the universal mirth,
  Cassandra-like, prognosticating woe;
They shook their heads, and doomed with dreadful words
To swift destruction the whole race of birds.

And a town-meeting was convened straightway
  To set a price upon the guilty heads
Of these marauders, who, in lieu of pay,
  Levied black-mail upon the garden beds
And cornfields, and beheld without dismay
  The awful scarecrow, with his fluttering shreds;
The skeleton that waited at their feast,
Whereby their sinful pleasure was increased.

Then from his house, a temple painted white,
  With fluted columns, and a roof of red,
The Squire came forth, august and splendid sight!
  Slowly descending, with majestic tread,
Three flights of steps, nor looking left nor right,
  Down the long street he walked, as one who said,
"A town that boasts inhabitants like me
Can have no lack of good society!"

The Parson, too, appeared, a man austere,
  The instinct of whose nature was to kill;
The wrath of God he preached from year to year,
  And read, with fervor, Edwards on the Will;
His favorite pastime was to slay the deer
  In Summer on some Adirondac hill;
E'en now, while walking down the rural lane,
He lopped the wayside lilies with his cane.

From the Academy, whose belfry crowned
  The hill of Science with its vane of brass,
Came the Preceptor, gazing idly round,
  Now at the clouds, and now at the green grass,
And all absorbed in reveries profound
  Of fair Almira in the upper class,
Who was, as in a sonnet he had said,
As pure as water, and as good as bread.

And next the Deacon issued from his door,
  In his voluminous neck-cloth, white as snow;
A suit of sable bombazine he wore;
  His form was ponderous, and his step was slow;
There never was so wise a man before;
  He seemed the incarnate "Well, I told you so!"
And to perpetuate his great renown
There was a street named after him in town.

These came together in the new town-hall,
  With sundry farmers from the region round.
The Squire presided, dignified and tall,
  His air impressive and his reasoning sound;
Ill fared it with the birds, both great and small;
  Hardly a friend in all that crowd they found,
But enemies enough, who every one
Charged them with all the crimes beneath the sun.

When they had ended, from his place apart,
  Rose the Preceptor, to redress the wrong,
And, trembling like a steed before the start,
  Looked round bewildered on the expectant throng;
Then thought of fair Almira, and took heart
  To speak out what was in him, clear and strong,
Alike regardless of their smile or frown,
And quite determined not to be laughed down.

"Plato, anticipating the Reviewers,
  From his Republic banished without pity
The Poets; in this little town of yours,
  You put to death, by means of a Committee,
The ballad-singers and the Troubadours,
  The street-musicians of the heavenly city,
The birds, who make sweet music for us all
In our dark hours, as David did for Saul.

"The thrush that carols at the dawn of day
  From the green steeples of the piny wood;
The oriole in the elm; the noisy jay,
  Jargoning like a foreigner at his food;
The bluebird balanced on some topmost spray,
  Flooding with melody the neighborhood;
Linnet and meadow-lark, and all the throng
That dwell in nests, and have the gift of song.

"You slay them all! and wherefore? for the gain
  Of a scant handful more or less of wheat,
Or rye, or barley, or some other grain,
  Scratched up at random by industrious feet,
Searching for worm or weevil after rain!
  Or a few cherries, that are not so sweet
As are the songs these uninvited guests,
Sing at their feast with comfortable breasts.

"Do you ne'er think what wondrous beings these?
  Do you ne'er think who made them and who taught
The dialect they speak, where melodies
  Alone are the interpreters of thought?
Whose household words are songs in many keys,
  Sweeter than instrument of man e'er caught!
Whose habitations in the tree-tops even
Are half-way houses on the road to heaven!

"Think, every morning when the sun peeps through
  The dim, leaf-latticed windows of the grove,
How jubilant the happy birds renew
  Their old, melodious madrigals of love!
And when you think of this, remember too
  'T is always morning somewhere, and above
The awakening continents; from shore to shore,
Somewhere the birds are singing evermore.

"Think of your woods and orchards without birds!
  Of empty nests that cling to boughs and beams
As in an idiot's brain remembered words
  Hang empty 'mid the cobwebs of his dreams!
Will bleat of flocks or bellowing of herds
  Make up for the lost music, when your teams
Drag home the stingy harvest, and no more
The feathered gleaners follow to your door?

"What! would you rather see the incessant stir
  Of insects in the windrows of the hay,
And hear the locust and the grasshopper
  Their melancholy hurdy-gurdies play?
Is this more pleasant to you than the whir
  Of meadow-lark, and her sweet roundelay,
Or twitter of little field-fares, as you take
Your nooning in the shade of bush and brake?

"You call them thieves and pillagers; but know,
  They are the wingéd wardens of your farms,
Who from the cornfields drive the insidious foe,
  And from your harvests keep a hundred harms;
Even the blackest of them all, the crow,
  Renders good service as your man-at-arms,
Crushing the beetle in his coat of mail,
And crying havoc on the slug and snail.

"How can I teach your children gentleness,
  And mercy to the weak, and reverence
For Life, which, in its weakness or excess,
  Is still a gleam of God's omnipotence,
Or Death, which, seeming darkness, is no less
  The selfsame light, although averted hence,
When by your laws, your actions, and your speech,
You contradict the very things I teach?"

With this he closed; and through the audience went
  A murmur, like the rustle of dead leaves;
The farmers laughed and nodded, and some bent
  Their yellow heads together like their sheaves;
Men have no faith in fine-spun sentiment
  Who put their trust in bullocks and in beeves.
The birds were doomed; and, as the record shows,
A bounty offered for the heads of crows.

There was another audience out of reach,
  Who had no voice nor vote in making laws,
But in the papers read his little speech,
  And crowned his modest temples with applause;
They made him conscious, each one more than each,
  He still was victor, vanquished in their cause.
Sweetest of all the applause he won from thee,
O fair Almira at the Academy!

And so the dreadful massacre began;
  O'er fields and orchards, and o'er woodland crests,
The ceaseless fusillade of terror ran.
  Dead fell the birds, with blood-stains on their breasts,
Or wounded crept away from sight of man,
  While the young died of famine in their nests;
A slaughter to be told in groans, not words,
The very St. Bartholomew of Birds!

The Summer came, and all the birds were dead;
  The days were like hot coals; the very ground
Was burned to ashes; in the orchards fed
  Myriads of caterpillars, and around
The cultivated fields and garden beds
  Hosts of devouring insects crawled, and found
No foe to check their march, till they had made
The land a desert without leaf or shade.

Devoured by worms, like Herod, was the town,
  Because, like Herod, it had ruthlessly
Slaughtered the Innocents. From the trees spun down
  The canker-worms upon the passers-by,
Upon each woman's bonnet, shawl, and gown,
  Who shook them off with just a little cry
They were the terror of each favorite walk,
The endless theme of all the village talk.

The farmers grew impatient but a few
  Confessed their error, and would not complain,
For after all, the best thing one can do
  When it is raining, is to let it rain.
Then they repealed the law, although they knew
  It would not call the dead to life again;
As school-boys, finding their mistake too late,
Draw a wet sponge across the accusing slate.

That year in Killingworth the Autumn came
  Without the light of his majestic look,
The wonder of the falling tongues of flame,
  The illumined pages of his Doom's-Day book.
A few lost leaves blushed crimson with their shame,
  And drowned themselves despairing in the brook,
While the wild wind went moaning everywhere,
Lamenting the dead children of the air!

But the next Spring a stranger sight was seen,
  A sight that never yet by bard was sung,
As great a wonder as it would have been
  If some dumb animal had found a tongue!
A wagon, overarched with evergreen,
  Upon whose boughs were wicker cages hung,
All full of singing birds, came down the street,
Filling the air with music wild and sweet.

From all the country round these birds were brought,
  By order of the town, with anxious quest,
And, loosened from their wicker prisons, sought
  In woods and fields the places they loved best,
Singing loud canticles, which many thought
  Were satires to the authorities addressed,
While others, listening in green lanes, averred
Such lovely music never had been heard!

But blither still and louder carolled they
  Upon the morrow, for they seemed to know
It was the fair Almira's wedding-day,
  And everywhere, around, above, below,
When the Preceptor bore his bride away,
  Their songs burst forth in joyous overflow,
And a new heaven bent over a new earth
Amid the sunny farms of Killingworth.

The Day is Done

The day is done, and the darkness
  Falls from the wings of Night,
As a feather is wafted downward
  From an eagle in his flight.

I see the lights of the village
  Gleam through the rain and the mist,
And a feeling of sadness comes o'er me
  That my soul cannot resist:

A feeling of sadness and longing,
  That is not akin to pain,
And resembles sorrow only
  As the mist resembles the rain.

Come, read to me some poem,
  Some simple and heartfelt lay,
That shall soothe this restless feeling,
  And banish the thoughts of day.

Not from the grand old masters,
  Not from the bards sublime,
Whose distant footsteps echo
  Through the corridors of Time.

For, like strains of martial music,
  Their mighty thoughts suggest
Life's endless toil and endeavor;
  And to-night I long for rest.

Read from some humbler poet,
  Whose songs gushed from his heart,
As showers from the clouds of summer,
  Or tears from the eyelids start;

Who, through long days of labor,
  And nights devoid of ease,
Still heard in his soul the music
  Of wonderful melodies.

Such songs have power to quiet
  The restless pulse of care,
And come like the benediction
  That follows after prayer.

Then read from the treasured volume
  The poem of thy choice,
And lend to the rhyme of the poet
  The beauty of thy voice.

And the night shall be filled with music
  And the cares, that infest the day,
Shall fold their tents, like the Arabs,
  And as silently steal away.

The Emperor's Bird's-Nest

Once the Emperor Charles of Spain,
  With his swarthy, grave commanders,
I forget in what campaign,
Long besieged, in mud and rain,
  Some old frontier town of Flanders.

Up and down the dreary camp,
  In great boots of Spanish leather,
Striding with a measured tramp,
These Hidalgos, dull and damp,
  Cursed the Frenchmen, cursed the weather.

Thus as to and fro they went,
  Over upland and through hollow,
Giving their impatience vent,
Perched upon the Emperor's tent,
  In her nest, they spied a swallow.

Yes, it was a swallow's nest,
  Built of clay and hair of horses,
Mane, or tail, or dragoon's crest,
Found on hedge-rows east and west,
  After skirmish of the forces.

Then an old Hidalgo said,
  As he twirled his gray mustachio,
"Sure this swallow overhead
Thinks the Emperor's tent a shed,
  And the Emperor but a Macho!"

Hearing his imperial name
  Coupled with those words of malice,
Half in anger, half in shame,
Forth the great campaigner came
  Slowly from his canvas palace.

"Let no hand the bird molest,"
  Said he solemnly, "nor hurt her!"
Adding then, by way of jest,
"Golondrina is my guest,
  'Tis the wife of some deserter!"

Swift as bowstring speeds a shaft,
  Through the camp was spread the rumor,
And the soldiers, as they quaffed
Flemish beer at dinner, laughed
  At the Emperor's pleasant humor.

So unharmed and unafraid
  Sat the swallow still and brooded,
Till the constant cannonade
Through the walls a breach had made,
  And the siege was thus concluded.

Then the army, elsewhere bent,
  Struck its tents as if disbanding,
Only not the Emperor's tent,
For he ordered, ere he went,
  Very curtly, "Leave it standing!"

So it stood there all alone,
  Loosely flapping, torn and tattered,
Till the brood was fledged and flown,
Singing o'er those walls of stone
  Which the cannon-shot had shattered.

Mina Loy

Brancusi's Golden Bird

The toy
become the aesthetic archetype

As if
  some patient peasant God
  had rubbed and rubbed
  the Alpha and Omega
  of Form
  into a lump of metal

  A naked orientation
  unwinged   unplumed
    —the ultimate rhythm
  has lopped the extremities
  of crest and claw
  from
  the nucleus of flight

  The absolute act
  of art
  conformed
  to continent sculpture
  —bare as the brow of Osiris—
  this breast of revelation

  an incandescent curve
  licked by chromatic flames
  in labyrinths of reflections

This gong
of polished hyperaesthesia
shrills with brass
as the aggressive light
strikes
its significance

The immaculate
conception
of the inaudible bird
occurs
in gorgeous reticence . . .

Herman Melville

The Man-of-War Hawk

Yon black man-of-war-hawk that wheels in the light
O'er the black ship's white sky-s'l, sunned cloud to the sight,
Have we low-flyers wings to ascend to his height?
No arrow can reach him; nor thought can attain
To the placid supreme in the sweep of his reign.

Monody

To have known him, to have loved him
  After loneness long;
And then to be estranged in life,
  And neither in the wrong;
And now for death to set his seal—
  Ease me, a little ease, my song!

By wintry hills his hermit-mound
  The sheeted snow-drifts drape,
And houseless there the snow-bird flits
  Beneath the fir-trees' crape:
Glazed now with ice the cloistral vine
  That hid the shyest grape.

George Meredith

The Lark Ascending

He rises and begins to round,
He drops the silver chain of sound
Of many links without a break,
In chirrup, whistle, slur and shake,
All intervolv'd and spreading wide,
Like water-dimples down a tide
Where ripple ripple overcurls
And eddy into eddy whirls;
A press of hurried notes that run
So fleet they scarce are more than one,
Yet changingly the trills repeat
And linger ringing while they fleet,
Sweet to the quick o' the ear, and dear
To her beyond the handmaid ear,
Who sits beside our inner springs,
Too often dry for this he brings,
Which seems the very jet of earth
At sight of sun, her music's mirth,
As up he wings the spiral stair,
A song of light, and pierces air
With fountain ardor, fountain play,
To reach the shining tops of day,
And drink in everything discern'd
An ecstasy to music turn'd,
Impell'd by what his happy bill
Disperses; drinking, showering still,
Unthinking save that he may give
His voice the outlet, there to live

Renew'd in endless notes of glee,
So thirsty of his voice is he,
For all to hear and all to know
That he is joy, awake, aglow,
The tumult of the heart to hear
Through pureness filter'd crystal-clear,
And know the pleasure sprinkled bright
By simple singing of delight,
Shrill, irreflective, unrestrain'd,
Rapt, ringing, on the jet sustain'd
Without a break, without a fall,
Sweet-silvery, sheer lyrical,
Perennial, quavering up the chord
Like myriad dews of sunny sward
That trembling into fulness shine,
And sparkle dropping argentine;
Such wooing as the ear receives
From zephyr caught in choric leaves
Of aspens when their chattering net
Is flush'd to white with shivers wet;
And such the water-spirit's chime
On mountain heights in morning's prime,
Too freshly sweet to seem excess,
Too animate to need a stress;
But wider over many heads
The starry voice ascending spreads,
Awakening, as it waxes thin,
The best in us to him akin;
And every face to watch him rais'd,
Puts on the light of children prais'd,
So rich our human pleasure ripes
When sweetness on sincereness pipes,
Though nought be promis'd from the seas,
But only a soft-ruffling breeze
Sweep glittering on a still content,
Serenity in ravishment.

For singing till his heaven fills,
'T is love of earth that he instils,
And ever winging up and up,
Our valley is his golden cup,
And he the wine which overflows
To lift us with him as he goes:
The woods and brooks, the sheep and kine
He is, the hills, the human line,
The meadows green, the fallows brown,
The dreams of labor in the town;
He sings the sap, the quicken'd veins;
The wedding song of sun and rains
He is, the dance of children, thanks
Of sowers, shout of primrose-banks,
And eye of violets while they breathe;
All these the circling song will wreathe,
And you shall hear the herb and tree,
The better heart of men shall see,
Shall feel celestially, as long
As you crave nothing save the song.
Was never voice of ours could say
Our inmost in the sweetest way,
Like yonder voice aloft, and link
All hearers in the song they drink:
Our wisdom speaks from failing blood,
Our passion is too full in flood,
We want the key of his wild note
Of truthful in a tuneful throat,
The song seraphically free
Of taint of personality,
So pure that it salutes the suns
The voice of one for millions,
In whom the millions rejoice
For giving their one spirit voice.

Yet men have we, whom we revere,
Now names, and men still housing here,
Whose lives, by many a battle-dint
Defaced, and grinding wheels on flint,
Yield substance, though they sing not, sweet
For song our highest heaven to greet:
Whom heavenly singing gives us new,
Enspheres them brilliant in our blue,
From firmest base to farthest leap,
Because their love of Earth is deep,
And they are warriors in accord
With life to serve and pass reward,
So touching purest and so heard
In the brain's reflex of yon bird;
Wherefore their soul in me, or mine,
Through self-forgetfulness divine,
In them, that song aloft maintains,
To fill the sky and thrill the plains
With showerings drawn from human stores,
As he to silence nearer soars,
Extends the world at wings and dome,
More spacious making more our home,
Till lost on his aërial rings
In light, and then the fancy sings.

John Milton

To the Nightingale

O Nightingale, that on yon blooming spray
Warblest at eve, when all the woods are still;
Thou with fresh hope the lover's heart dost fill,
While the jolly hours lead on propitious May.
Thy liquid notes that close the eye of day,
First heard before the shallow cuckoo's bill,
Portend success in love; O, if Jove's will
Have link'd that amorous power to thy soft lay,
Now timely sing, ere the rude bird of hate
Foretell my hopeless doom in some grove nigh;
As thou from year to year hast sung too late
For my relief, yet had'st no reason why:
Whether the Muse, or Love, call thee his mate,
Both them I serve, and of their train am I.

Edgar Allan Poe

The Raven

Once upon a midnight dreary, while I pondered, weak and weary,
Over many a quaint and curious volume of forgotten lore,
While I nodded, nearly napping, suddenly there came a tapping,
As of some one gently rapping, rapping at my chamber door.
"'Tis some visitor," I muttered, "tapping at my chamber door—
        Only this and nothing more."

Ah, distinctly I remember it was in the bleak December,
And each separate dying ember wrought its ghost upon the floor.
Eagerly I wished the morrow;—vainly I had sought to borrow
From my books surcease of sorrow—sorrow for the lost Lenore—
For the rare and radiant maiden whom the angels name Lenore—
        Nameless here for evermore.

And the silken sad uncertain rustling of each purple curtain
Thrilled me—filled me with fantastic terrors never felt before;
So that now, to still the beating of my heart, I stood repeating
"'Tis some visitor entreating entrance at my chamber door—
Some late visitor entreating entrance at my chamber door;—
        This it is, and nothing more."

Presently my soul grew stronger; hesitating then no longer,
"Sir," said I, "or Madam, truly your forgiveness I implore;
But the fact is I was napping, and so gently you came rapping,
And so faintly you came tapping, tapping at my chamber door,
That I scarce was sure I heard you"—here I opened wide the
 door;——
        Darkness there and nothing more.

Deep into that darkness peering, long I stood there wondering, fearing,
Doubting, dreaming dreams no mortal ever dared to dream before;
But the silence was unbroken, and the stillness gave no token,
And the only word there spoken was the whispered word, "Lenore!"
This I whispered, and an echo murmured back the word, "Lenore!"
                              Merely this, and nothing more.

Back into the chamber turning, all my soul within me burning,
Soon again I heard a tapping somewhat louder than before.
"Surely," said I, "surely that is something at my window lattice;
Let me see, then, what thereat is, and this mystery explore;—
Let my heart be still a moment and this mystery explore;—
                              'Tis the wind and nothing more!"

Open here I flung the shutter, when, with many a flirt and flutter,
In there stepped a stately raven of the saintly days of yore;
Not the least obeisance made he; not a minute stopped or stayed he;
But, with mien of lord or lady, perched above my chamber door—
Perched upon a bust of Pallas just above my chamber door—
                              Perched, and sat, and nothing more.

Then this ebony bird beguiling my sad fancy into smiling,
By the grave and stern decorum of the countenance it wore,
"Though thy crest be shorn and shaven, thou," I said, "art sure no craven,
Ghastly grim and ancient raven wandering from the Nightly shore—
Tell me what thy lordly name is on the Night's Plutonian shore!"
                              Quoth the raven "Nevermore."

Much I marvelled this ungainly fowl to hear discourse so plainly,
Though its answer little meaning—little relevancy bore;
For we cannot help agreeing that no living human being
Ever yet was blessed with seeing bird above his chamber door—
Bird or beast upon the sculptured bust above his chamber door,
                              With such name as "Nevermore."

But the raven, sitting lonely on the placid bust, spoke only
That one word, as if his soul in that one word he did outpour.
Nothing farther then he uttered—not a feather then he fluttered—
Till I scarcely more than muttered "Other friends have flown
  before—
On the morrow *he* will leave me, as my hopes have flown before."
                    Then the bird said "Nevermore."

Startled at the stillness broken by reply so aptly spoken,
"Doubtless," said I, "what it utters is its only stock and store
Caught from some unhappy master whom unmerciful Disaster
Followed fast and followed faster till his songs one burden bore—
Till the dirges of his Hope that melancholy burden bore
                    Of "Never—nevermore."

But the raven still beguiling all my sad soul into smiling,
Straight I wheeled a cushioned seat in front of bird, and bust and
  door;
Then, upon the velvet sinking, I betook myself to linking
Fancy unto fancy, thinking what this ominous bird of yore—
What this grim, ungainly, ghastly, gaunt and ominous bird of yore
                    Meant in croaking "Nevermore."

This I sat engaged in guessing, but no syllable expressing
To the fowl whose fiery eyes now burned into my bosom's core;
This and more I sat divining, with my head at ease reclining
On the cushion's velvet lining that the lamp-light gloated o'er,
But whose velvet violet lining with the lamp-light gloating o'er,
                    She shall press, ah, nevermore!

Then, methought, the air grew denser, perfumed from an unseen
  censer
Swung by angels whose foot-falls tinkled on the tufted floor.
"Wretch," I cried, "thy God hath lent thee—by these angels he
  hath sent thee
Respite—respite and nepenthe from thy memories of Lenore!
Quaff, oh quaff this kind nepenthe and forget this lost Lenore!"
                    Quoth the raven "Nevermore."

"Prophet!" said I, "thing of evil!—prophet still, if bird or devil!—
Whether Tempter sent, or whether tempest tossed thee here
    ashore,
Desolate yet all undaunted, on this desert land enchanted—
On this home by Horror haunted—tell me truly, I implore—
Is there—*is* there balm in Gilead?—tell me—tell me, I implore!"
                                Quoth the raven "Nevermore."

"Prophet!" said I, "thing of evil!—prophet still, if bird or devil!
By that Heaven that bends above us—by that God we both
    adore—
Tell this soul with sorrow laden if, within the distant Aidenn,
It shall clasp a sainted maiden whom the angels name Lenore—
Clasp a rare and radiant maiden whom the angels name Lenore."
                                Quoth the raven "Nevermore."

"Be that word our sign of parting, bird or fiend!" I shrieked,
    upstarting—
"Get thee back into the tempest and the Night's Plutonian shore!
Leave no black plume as a token of that lie thy soul hath spoken!
Leave my loneliness unbroken!—quit the bust above my door!
Take thy beak from out my heart, and take thy form from off my
    door!"
                                Quoth the raven "Nevermore."

And the raven, never flitting, still is sitting, still is sitting
On the pallid bust of Pallas just above my chamber door;
And his eyes have all the seeming of a demon's that is dreaming,
And the lamp-light o'er him streaming throws his shadow on the
    floor;
And my soul from out that shadow that lies floating on the floor
                                Shall be lifted—nevermore!

Thomas Ravenscroft

The Three Ravens

There were three ravens sat on a tree,
  Downe a downe, hay down, hay downe,
There were three ravens sat on a tree,
  With a downe
There were three ravens sat on a tree,
They were as blacke as they might be,
  With a downe derrie, derrie, derrie, downe, downe.

The one of them said to his mate,
"Where shall we our breakfast take?"

"Downe in yonder greene field,
There lies a knight slain under his shield.

"His hounds they lie downe at his feete,
So well they can their Master keepe.

"His hawkes they flie so eagerly,
There's no fowle dare him come nie."

Downe there comes a fallow doe,
As great with yong as she might goe.

She lift up his bloudy hed,
And kist his wounds that were so red.

She got him up upon her backe,
And carried him to earthen lake.

She buried him before the prime,
She was dead herselfe ere even-song time.

God send every gentleman,
Such hawkes, such hounds, and such a leman.

William Shakespeare

The Phoenix and the Turtle

Let the bird of loudest lay,
On the sole Arabian tree,
Herald sad and trumpet be,
To whose sound chaste wings obey.

But thou shrieking harbinger,
Foul precurrer of the fiend,
Augur of the fever's end,
To this troop come thou not near!

From this session interdict
Every fowl of tyrant wing,
Save the eagle, feather'd king:
Keep the obsequy so strict.

Let the priest in surplice white,
That defunctive music can,
Be the death-divining swan,
Lest the requiem lack his right.

And thou treble-dated crow,
That thy sable gender makest
With the breath thou givest and takest,
'Mongst our mourners shalt thou go.

Here the anthem doth commence:
Love and constancy is dead;
Phoenix and the turtle fled
In a mutual flame from hence.

So they lov'd, as love in twain
Had the essence but in one;
Two distincts, division none:
Number there in love was slain.

Hearts remote, yet not asunder;
Distance and no space was seen
'Twixt this turtle and his queen:
But in them it were a wonder.

So between them love did shine,
That the turtle saw his right
Flaming in the phoenix' sight;
Either was the other's mine.

Property was thus appalled,
That the self was not the same;
Single nature's double name
Neither two nor one was called.

Reason, in itself confounded,
Saw division grow together,
To themselves yet either neither,
Simple were so well compounded;

That it cried, How true a twain
Seemeth this concordant one!
Love has reason, reason none,
If what parts can so remain.

Whereupon it made this threne
To the phoenix and the dove,
Co-supremes and stars of love,
As chorus to their tragic scene.

Threnos

Beauty, truth, and rarity,
Grace in all simplicity,
Here enclos'd, in cinders lie.

Death is now the phoenix' nest;
And the turtle's loyal breast
To eternity doth rest,

Leaving no posterity:
'Twas not their infirmity,
It was married chastity.

Truth may seem but cannot be;
Beauty brag, but 'tis not she;
Truth and beauty buried be.

To this urn let those repair
That are either true or fair;
For these dead birds sigh a prayer.

Wallace Stevens

Bantams in Pine-Woods

Chieftain Iffucan of Azcan in caftan
Of tan with henna hackles, halt!

Damned universal cock, as if the sun
Was blackamoor to bear your blazing tail.

Fat! Fat! Fat! Fat! I am the personal.
Your world is you. I am my world.

You ten-foot poet among inchlings. Fat!
Begone! An inchling bristles in these pines,

Bristles, and points their Appalachian tangs,
And fears not portly Azcan nor his hoos.

Thirteen Ways of Looking at a Blackbird

I
Among twenty snowy mountains,
The only moving thing
Was the eye of the blackbird.

II
I was of three minds,
Like a tree
In which there are three blackbirds.

III
The blackbird whirled in the autumn winds.
It was a small part of the pantomime.

IV
A man and a woman
Are one.
A man and a woman and a blackbird
Are one.

V
I do not know which to prefer,
The beauty of inflections
Or the beauty of innuendoes,
The blackbird whistling
Or just after.

VI
Icicles filled the long window
With barbaric glass.
The shadow of the blackbird
Crossed it, to and fro.
The mood
Traced in the shadow
An indecipherable cause.

VII
O thin men of Haddam,
Why do you imagine golden birds?
Do you not see how the blackbird
Walks around the feet
Of the women about you?

VIII
I know noble accents
And lucid, inescapable rhythms;
But I know, too,
That the blackbird is involved
In what I know.

IX
When the blackbird flew out of sight,
It marked the edge
Of one of many circles.

X
At the sight of blackbirds
Flying in a green light,
Even the bawds of euphony
Would cry out sharply.

XI
He rode over Connecticut
In a glass coach.
Once, a fear pierced him,
In that he mistook
The shadow of his equipage
For blackbirds.

XII
The river is moving.
The blackbird must be flying.

XIII
It was evening all afternoon.
It was snowing
And it was going to snow.
The blackbird sat
In the cedar-limbs.

Alfred, Lord Tennyson

The Eagle

He clasps the crag with crooked hands;
Close to the sun in lonely lands,
Ring'd with the azure world, he stands.

The wrinkled sea beneath him crawls;
He watches from his mountain walls,
And like a thunderbolt he falls.

Henry David Thoreau

The Shrike

Hark! Hark! from out the thickest fog
Warbles with might and main
The fearless shrike, as all agog
To find in fog his gain.

His steady sails he never furls
At any time o' year,
And, perched now on Winter's curls,
He whistles in his ear.

Henry Vaughan

The Bird

Hither thou com'st. The busy wind all night
Blew through thy lodging, where thy own warm wing
Thy pillow was. Many a sullen storm,
For which coarse man seems much the fitter born,
     Rained on thy bed
     And harmless head;

And now, as fresh and cheerful as the light,
Thy little heart in early hymns doth sing
Unto that Providence, whose unseen arm
Curbed them, and clothed thee well and warm.
All things that be praise Him; and had
Their lesson taught them when first made.

So hills and valleys into singing break;
And though poor stones have neither speech nor tongue,
While active winds and streams both run and speak,
Yet stones are deep in admiration.
Thus praise and prayer here beneath the sun
Make lesser mornings, when the great are done.

For each inclosed spirit is a star
  Inlight'ning his own little sphere,
Whose light, though fetcht and borrowed from far,
  Both mornings makes and evenings there.

But as these birds of light make a land glad,
  Chirping their solemn matins on each tree;
  So in the shades of night some dark fowls be,
Whose heavy notes make all that hear them sad.

The turtle then in palm-trees mourns,
  While owls and satyrs howl:
The pleasant land to brimstone turns,
  And all her streams grow foul.

Brightness and mirth, and love and faith, all fly,
Till the day-spring breaks forth again from high.

Cock-Crowing

Father of lights! what sunny seed,
What glance of day hast Thou confined
Into this bird? To all the breed
This busy ray Thou hast assigned;
  Their magnetism works all night,
  And dreams of Paradise and light.

Their eyes watch for the morning hue;
Their little grain, expelling night,
So shines and sings, as if it knew
The path unto the house of light:
  It seems their candle, howe'er done,
  Was tined and lighted at the sun.

If such a tincture, such a touch,
So firm a longing can empower,
Shall Thy own image think it much
To watch for Thy appearing hour?
  If a mere blast so fill the sail,
  Shall not the breath of God prevail?

O Thou immortal Light and Heat!
Whose hand so shines through all this frame,
That by the beauty of the seat
We plainly see who made the same!
  Seeing Thy seed abides in me,
  Dwell Thou in it, and I in Thee.

To sleep without Thee is to die;
Yea, 't is a death partakes of hell:
For where Thou dost not close the eye,
It never opens, I can tell.
  In such a dark Egyptian border,
  The shades of death dwell, and disorder.

If joys, and hopes, and earnest throes,
And hearts whose pulse beats still for light.
Are given to birds, who but Thee knows
A love-sick soul's exalted flight?
  Can souls be tracked by any eye
  But His who gave them wings to fly?

Only this veil which Thou hast broke,
And must be broken yet in me:
This veil, I say, is all the cloak
And cloud which shadows me from Thee.
  This veil Thy full-eyed love denies,
  And only gleams and fractions spies.

Oh, take it off. Make no delay.
But brush me with Thy light that I
May shine unto a perfect day,
And warm me at Thy glorious eye.
  Oh, take it off: or till it flee,
  Though with no lily, stay with me.

Walt Whitman

The Dalliance of the Eagles

Skirting the river road, (my forenoon walk, my rest,)
Skyward in air a sudden muffled sound, the dalliance of the eagles,
The rushing amorous contact high in space together,
The clinching interlocking claws, a living, fierce, gyrating wheel,
Four beating wings, two beaks, a swirling mass tight grappling,
In tumbling turning clustering loops, straight downward falling,
Till o'er the river pois'd, the twain yet one, a moment's lull,
A motionless still balance in the air, then parting, talons loosing,
Upward again on slow-firm pinions slanting, their separate diverse
   flight,
She hers, he his, pursuing.

My Canary Bird

Did we count great, O soul, to penetrate the themes of mighty
  books,
Absorbing deep and full from thoughts, plays, speculations?
But now from thee to me, caged bird, to feel thy joyous warble,
Filling the air, the lonesome room, the long forenoon,
Is it not just as great, O soul?

To the Man-of-War-Bird

Thou who hast slept all night upon the storm,
Waking renew'd on thy prodigious pinions,
(Burst the wild storm? above it thou ascended'st,
And rested on the sky, thy slave that cradled thee,)
Now a blue point, far, far in heaven floating,
As to the light emerging here on deck I watch thee,
(Myself a speck, a point on the world's floating vast.)

Far, far at sea,
After the night's fierce drifts have strewn the shore with wrecks,
With re-appearing day as now so happy and serene,
The rosy and elastic dawn, the flashing sun,
The limpid spread of air cerulean,
Thou also re-appearest.

Thou born to match the gale, (thou art all wings,)
To cope with heaven and earth and sea and hurricane,
Thou ship of air that never furl'st thy sails,
Days, even weeks untired and onward, through spaces, realms
    gyrating,
At dusk that look'st on Senegal, at morn America,
That sport'st amid the lightning-flash and thunder-cloud,
In them, in thy experiences, had'st thou my soul,
What joys! what joys were thine!

William Carlos Williams

Pastoral

The little sparrows
hop ingenuously
about the pavement
quarreling
with sharp voices
over those things
that interest them.
But we who are wiser
shut ourselves in
on either hand
and no one knows
whether we think good
or evil.
        Meanwhile,
the old man who goes about
gathering dog-lime
walks in the gutter
without looking up
and his tread
is more majestic than
that of the Episcopal minister
approaching the pulpit
of a Sunday.
        These things
astonish me beyond words.

William Wordsworth

The Contrast—The Parrot and the Wren

I
Within her gilded cage confined,
I saw a dazzling Belle,
A Parrot of that famous kind
Whose name is NON-PAREIL.

Like beads of glossy jet her eyes;
And, smoothed by Nature's skill,
With pearl or gleaming agate vies
Her finely-curved bill.

Her plumy mantle's living hues
In mass opposed to mass,
Outshine the splendour that imbues
The robes of pictured glass.

And, sooth to say, an apter Mate
Did never tempt the choice
Of feathered Thing most delicate
In figure and in voice.

But, exiled from Australian bowers,
And singleness her lot,
She trills her song with tutored powers,
Or mocks each casual note.

No more of pity for regrets
With which she may have striven!
Now but in wantonness she frets,
Or spite, if cause be given;

Arch, volatile, a sportive bird
By social glee inspired;
Ambitious to be seen or heard,
And pleased to be admired!

II
This moss-lined shed, green, soft, and dry,
Harbours a self-contented Wren,
Not shunning man's abode, though shy,
Almost as thought itself, of human ken.

Strange places, coverts unendeared,
She never tried; the very nest
In which this Child of Spring was reared,
Is warmed, thro' winter, by her feathery breast.

To the bleak winds she sometimes gives
A slender unexpected strain;
Proof that the hermitess still lives,
Though she appear not, and be sought in vain.

Say, Dora! tell me, by yon placid moon,
If called to choose between the favoured pair,
Which would you be,—the bird of the saloon,
By lady-fingers tended with nice care,
Caressed, applauded, upon dainties fed,
Or Nature's DARKLING of this mossy shed?

William Butler Yeats

His Phoenix

There is a queen in China, or maybe it's in Spain,
And birthdays and holidays such praises can be heard
Of her unblemished lineaments, a whiteness with no stain,
That she might be that sprightly girl trodden by a bird;
And there's a score of duchesses, surpassing womankind,
Or who have found a painter to make them so for pay
And smooth out stain and blemish with the elegance of his mind:
I knew a phoenix in my youth, so let them have their day.

The young men every night applaud their Gaby's laughing eye,
And Ruth St. Denis had more charm although she had poor luck;
From nineteen hundred nine or ten, Pavlova's had the cry,
And there's a player in the States who gathers up her cloak
And flings herself out of the room when Juliet would be bride
With all a woman's passion, a child's imperious way,
And there are—but no matter if there are scores beside:
I knew a phoenix in my youth, so let them have their day.

There's Margaret and Marjorie and Dorothy and Nan,
A Daphne and a Mary who live in privacy;
One's had her fill of lovers, another's had but one,
Another boasts, "I pick and choose and have but two or three."
If head and limb have beauty and the instep's high and light
They can spread out what sail they please for all I have to say,
Be but the breakers of men's hearts or engines of delight:
I knew a phoenix in my youth, so let them have their day.

There'll be that crowd, that barbarous crowd, through all the
    centuries,
And who can say but some young belle may walk and talk men
    wild
Who is my beauty's equal, though that my heart denies,
But not the exact likeness, the simplicity of a child,
And that proud look as though she had gazed into the burning
    sun,
And all the shapely body no tittle gone astray.
I mourn for that most lonely thing; and yet God's will be done:
I knew a phoenix in my youth, so let them have their day.